Ashes at the Coffee Shop, Resurrection at the Bus Stop

*Sermons for Lent and Easter
Based on the Gospel Texts*

Mary Austin

CSS Publishing Company, Inc.
Lima, Ohio

ASHES AT THE COFFEE SHOP, RESURRECTION AT THE BUS STOP

FIRST EDITION
Copyright © 2020
by CSS Publishing Co., Inc.

Library of Congress Cataloging-in-Publication Data:

Names: Austin, Mary, 1954- author. Title: Ashes at the coffee shop, resurrection at the bus stop: sermons for Lent and Easter based on the gospel text / Mary Austin. Description: First edition. | Lima, Ohio: CSS Publishing Company, Inc., [2020] | Summary: "Lectionary Sermons for the Lent and Easter season by Mary Austin"-- Provided by publisher. Identifiers: LCCN 2020007265 | ISBN 9780788029974 (paperback) | ISBN 9780788029981 (ebook) Subjects: LCSH: Bible. Gospels--Sermons. | Eastertide--Sermons. | Lenten sermons. | Common lectionary (1992) Classification: LCC BS2555.54 .A93 2020 | DDC 252/.62--dc23 LC record available at https://lccn.loc.gov/2020007265

For more information about CSS Publishing Company resources, visit our website at www.csspub.com, email us at csr@csspub.com, or call (800) 241-4056.

e-book:
ISBN-13: 978-0-7880-2998-1
ISBN-10: 0-7880-2998-3

ISBN-13: 978-0-7880-2997-4
ISBN-10: 0-7880-2997-5

PRINTED DIGITALLY

To the people of Gaithersburg Presbyterian Church, who embody community, and the people of Westminster Church of Detroit who taught me so much.

Contents

Ash Wednesday

Matthew 6:1-6, 16-21

Ashes At Starbucks

This passage from Matthew is an odd choice from the lectionary, for the day we have the most public display of our Christian faith. "Beware of practicing your piety before others in order to be seen by them," Jesus says. Good advice. Then we go ahead and mark our foreheads with ashes for everyone to see. If we stop for bread and milk on the way home or go to an early service and wear our ashes to work, if we stop by for some drive-thru ashes, we can't help but advertise our faith. Most days of the year, no one knows from the outside that we're Christians. We don't wear a hijab, like some of our Muslim neighbors, or yarmulkes, like some of our Jewish neighbors. But on Ash Wednesday, everyone at the grocery store, the office, or Starbucks knows our faith.

Are we doing exactly what Jesus warned against?

Or are we just getting our outside to match the inside?

The sign of ashes on the outside reminds us who we are on the inside.

Maybe you already know a lot about ashes.

If you lost a loved one recently, or if you've been sick, or if you live with pain that won't go away, you know all about the taste of ashes in your life. If you're struggling with finances, if you're working hard every day and feel like you're getting nowhere, you know about dreams turning to ashes. If your child has gone off somewhere you can't reach them, then you know the feeling of ashes.

In our world, the taste of ashes is everywhere.

Every day seems to bring another shooting, at a courthouse or church, parking garage, or a school. We excel at tearing people down with videos and Twitter.

The ashes are all around us... and within us.

Maybe it's a relief to wear them on your forehead this year. You're ready for some mourning and turning back to God.

In this text, the traditional one for Ash Wednesday and the start of Lent, we hear Jesus talking about the traditional practices of Jewish faith of his day — fasting, prayer, and giving money to the poor. In his tradition, these were the big three. He's not urging people to *do* these things — he's assuming they will. It goes without saying that he expects them to practice their faith. But, as always, Jesus is concerned about *how* we do things.

In our time, the way we practice our faith is different — it could be teaching Sunday school, or setting up communion, or welcoming guests to the church. It could be what church people consider sacred time — serving on a committee. Some people find the touch of the Spirit through being in a small group, meditating, doing yoga, walking prayer, or praying with music. It's all good — and still Jesus invites us to make a radical shift in how we do them.

Jesus tells us to lay aside any notion of impressing one another, or even being pleased with ourselves. Don't make a performance out of your faith, he tells us. Don't worry about the prayer you're going to say for a group, and whether or not the words are right. Don't count up your hours working at the soup kitchen. Don't tell people that no one can clean the church kitchen like you can. Work behind the scenes, in the same way that God works invisibly. Get out of the game of constantly assessing, weighing, counting, measuring, judging others and ourselves.

Part of our human nature is that we can only focus really well on a few things at a time. It's hard to have two full-time jobs. It's difficult to date two people seriously at the same time — let alone be married to more than one. We can concentrate on how well we're doing — or how well other people are doing — or we can focus on our inner connection with God.

Hasn't this happened to all of us?

We have a fabulous spiritual moment, and we're basking in the glow of how great God is or how spiritual we are, and then we're rude to a store clerk, or yell at a family member, or get impatient with a neighbor.

We're always called to turn back, to keep turning toward God. We're always reminded to make the inside match the outside. No one shows us the truth of who we are like the people who bug us, or our own children and partners. It's easy to look great to the outside world. Jesus is calling us to let that go, and to concentrate on the connection to God.

To remind us of how fleeting everything is, we have this mark of ashes on our foreheads.

This mark is for us — a sign that our lives are ashes, as well as joy, and that the ashes are not the final word. When we look in the mirror today and catch sight of our foreheads, when we wash our faces tonight, as we go through Lent and remember the shadow on our foreheads, the mark on the outside reminds us of who we are on the inside. Even in the ashes, we belong to God. We belong to the God who comes into the ashes and brings out life. The God who has the last word over our limitations, over death, and sin, and everything in this world.

The ashes proclaim on the outside the deepest truth we know on the inside. We are people of faith, on a spiritual journey. We're marked with our prayer to turn toward God, and with God's promise that there *is* more than ashes. Amen.

Things That Open

Now that we can watch all of our favorite shows on DVR, Amazon Prime, Netflix, or any one of a zillion ways, we no longer have the experience we used to have, of watching something and then turning to a friend and saying, "What did he say?", "What was that mumble?" or "Where are they going?" Anything we miss, we can just rewind and see again.

This story from Mark's gospel, starting us off in the season of Lent, is one we want to rewind, again and again. A lot — a *lot* — happens in these seven verses. Mark is known for being the most spare of all the gospels. He has way less detailed than Matthew and Luke, and he wrote with a kind of "just the facts" approach. In these few verses, Jesus was baptized, made his way into the wilderness, and started his public ministry.

Jesus might want to rewind, too.

One minute, he was being baptized by his cousin John. Then the heavens are torn apart. Before he had time to even think about that, God's Spirit descended on him like a dove, a sign of peace. The next minute, that same Spirit drove him into the wilderness. His forty days in the wilderness gave shape to our forty days of Lent.

It's not clear, in Mark's bare bones telling of the story, if anyone besides Jesus saw the Spirit descending on Jesus. We can't even tell if anyone else heard the voice speaking with Him. In Advent, we heard the prophet Isaiah call out to God, *O that you would tear open the heavens and come down.* (Isaiah 64:1) Now God has done that very thing. The God who was far away is now a lot closer. Mark wanted to be sure we knew that, in Jesus' life, God is moving closer to humankind. The door is open for us, too.

This same odd thing happens in Jesus' death. The curtain in the temple — the divider between God and people — was torn in two. The division between God and people was torn away. As scholar Donald Juel said, "the protecting barriers are gone and… God, unwilling to be confined to sacred spaces, is on the loose in our own realm…" (from *A Master of Surprise*, (Minneapolis, Fortress Press, 35-35))

The presence of Jesus is a door opener. At his baptism, at his death, and in our world, too.

In Lent, we follow Jesus into the wilderness. We follow his forty days in the desert with our own forty days of Lent. When we have the patience and the courage to follow Jesus into the wilderness, doors open for us, too. Life may be ripped open, or we may choose the opening, and we find God in both.

Following Jesus into this desert, we realize that we have temptations, too. When we stop and focus on God, we see how addicted we are to our screens, to the instant amusement of our phones, to the quick hit of adrenaline as we win a game online or score a bargain on a purchase.

Like Jesus, we have wild beasts in our lives. They take different forms for us. We are surrounded by the wild beasts of incivility, of prejudice, of demeaning others, of language that tears down instead of building up. There's plenty of wild rage and anger around us — and within us. When we make friends with our own wild beasts, whatever their shape, we can be much more useful to God. The things that divide us from God get torn away, and we are connected to God in deeper and deeper ways.

Everyone has had a time when life rips you open and empties you out into a desert of confusion… or pain… or change. We choose to deal with an addiction, or to take a step toward a long-held dream. We work up the courage to live differently, even when it's hard and people don't understand. We make a choice to end one chapter or begin another, to start a relationship or end one. All of those things open doors in our lives.

None of this is easy — whether it happens to us, or whether we choose it.

I remember on the way to the hospital, when it was time to have my first child, thinking, "On second thought, I changed my mind." Nope, too late.

Our lives were about to be ripped open by the joyful, tiring, exasperating, soul-changing work of being parents. You've had similar experiences when you go into the military, start a new job or end a job, dive deeply into a committed relationship or realize you need to end one. Things are ripped open in our lives by choice, or by events that happen to us. It happens through joys that demand extra from us, and through sorrows that leave us broken.

All of those ripped places are places where God comes into our lives, even more deeply than ever before.

It can happen at church, too, when we start a new program, or have to let go of a familiar one. We can feel like something is being ripped away whenever the church changes. It happens when we take on a leadership role in the church or community and see a beloved organization in a new way. Some people never recover from that kind of ripping because it's so painful to see how the sausage is made.

Physician and storyteller Dr. Rachel Naomi Remen said that one her patients, terminally ill with cancer once told her, "I've noticed that there are two kinds of people in the world — those who are afraid, and those who are alive." (from *My Grandfather's Blessings*)

Fear is normal when a new door opens, or when something is torn open. We want to go back. And yet Jesus reminds us here that we can only go forward. The old chapter has already been torn away, and we have no choice but to go on to the new. Even Jesus can't stay in the river, basking in his baptism, and feeling the grace of the Spirit. He has to go out into the wilderness, for the first chapter of his work.

In Jesus, in his life and example, God opens a door for us. God tears open the heavens and comes fully into our lives.

When life is ready to rip us open, when we're ready to open a new door, we are meant to remember our baptism. Remember that God is alive in our world, in all our deserts and all our successes, in all our new chapters and all our endings.

God opens the door for us to come closer — this Lent, and always.

In turn, God wants us to be door openers, too, so others can see God, too.

In the name of Jesus, Amen.

Jesus Gets A Business Card

There's a lot of talk these days in the non-profit and business world these days about "elevator speeches." If we run into someone in an elevator, and they ask about our cause, our start-up business, or our church, we should be able to give a quick summary, short enough to fit the elevator ride. When people ask about my church, I say something like: "Gaithersburg is a multi-cultural church with members from over thirty countries, so living together is fun and full of things to learn." If we're going to the twentieth floor, I can say a little more!

Jesus, always the master communicator, is giving the disciples his version of an elevator speech here. This is the core of what he's trying to teach them.

We can feel the focus of the gospel shift now.

The first eight chapters of Mark make the case for who Jesus is. He shows us and tells us by his healings, his meals, his teaching, in everything he says and does. Now, the story shifts, and Jesus begins to make his way toward Jerusalem. As he goes, he asks his friends "what are people saying about me?" (Mark 8:29) They offer up various answers, no doubt leaving out the negative ones. And then he asks who they think he is. You can imagine the looks that passed between them — the nod of a head, the quirk of an eyebrow as if to say: you tell him; no, you tell him. How many nights around the campfire, we wonder, did they talk about this? How many meals when they sat in the background and watched, how many healings when they saw the change with their own eyes, made them wonder, and talk about this when Jesus wasn't around.

Now Peter steps up with the answer he must have been wondering and weighing and thinking about: the Messiah.

And he's got it half right.

We get it half right, too. A lot of the popular religion we find in the media and in Christian bookstores means well. The TV preachers talk about a life of deeper faith, but it looks a lot like the American success story. Shiny, well-fed people with seemingly perfect lives try to convince us that if we're true Christians, we'll never struggle again. Money will pile up so fast we don't know what to do, struggles with alcohol or drugs will be gone with no effort… calories won't exist… our aches and pains will vanish… and bad bosses will turn into pussycats. Certainly, we'll never swear at other drivers in traffic or lose our tempers at home.

It all sounds so good that we want to believe it, and yet part of us knows it's too good to be true.

Once while I was in seminary, a well-known preacher came to address the students during the morning chapel time. We gathered, expectantly, on those wooden pews that had seen a lot of preachers come and go. As we listened, he talked for a long time about his perfect marriage of 35 years, and his five children, four of whom were leading perfect lives. He went on so long that a friend of mine leaned over and said, "Aren't you just praying the fifth kid is a Hare Krishna somewhere?"

As author Brennan Manning says, "Most of the descriptions of the victorious life do not match the reality of my own. [Things you read and hear] create the impression that once Jesus is acknowledged as Lord, the Christian life becomes a picnic on a green lawn — marriage blossoms into connubial bliss, physical health flourishes, acne disappears, and sinking careers suddenly soar. The victorious life is proclaimed to mean that everyone is a winner. An attractive twenty-year-old accepts Jesus and becomes Miss America, a floundering lawyer conquers alcoholism and whips F. Lee Bailey in court, a tenth round draft choice for the Green Bay Packers goes to the Pro Bowl. Miracles occur, conversions abound, church attendance skyrockets, ruptured relationships get healed, shy people become gregarious and the [insert your team here] win the World Series." (*The Ragamuffin Gospel*, by Brennan Manning)

If we don't get this kind of perfection, we feel like we missed out on the life of faith.

But Jesus is saying, no, you have it all wrong. It's the struggles, the taking up your burdens and the burdens of the world, that give life to faith.

Peter has this happy vision of faith, too — and he can't imagine a messiah who will suffer and die. For him, that's a failure. Peter tries to rebuke Jesus — the same word the gospel uses for casting out demons. And Jesus comes right back at him. He has to understand this to get it. Jesus rebukes Peter — again, the same word for casting out a demon.

If we want to follow — and Jesus is clear that we have a choice — this is the path.

So, if it's not perfect day after perfect day, what does it mean to follow Jesus in our world? That's the mystery our faith leads us to explore, day after day, year after year. That's the question we ask Jesus, as we live our everyday faith.

Jesus is telling us here who he is — and who we should be, too. He's talking about the core of his work — and the core of our life as disciples. We live our faith in the answer to his questions.

Who do you say that I am, Jesus asks? Can you follow me? Can you take up your cross: face the burdens of your life, and carry the cares of the world? He has these questions for us.

We have questions, too.

Faith demands that we ask ourselves these things.

Does my work use the talents God gave me? By work, I mean however we spend our days: raising kids, paid work, volunteer work.

Do my relationships show the love and grace of God? In the way I talk to my friends, my neighbors, my partner, my kids, am I talking to the face of God in them?

Does my life show evidence of God?

Am I growing in some way, or have I gotten stuck?

What do I regret?

If I had three months to live, what would I want to fit into my life?

These questions, and others like them, pointing us to what really matters, and to where God would have us go. They are signposts, showing us where we're unhappy… missing something… going too fast…. They lead us into the mystery of how we follow God in the places we are, with the gifts we have.

And at the center of it all, there are questions that give meaning to all the others. Who do you say that I am? Can you pick up your cross and follow me? Can you face your burdens, and care for the needs of others?

As one writer says, "As life picks up speed and I clock more days and weeks and years, I accumulate more suffering. The human tendency seems to be to fight the difficult parts of life, as if by resisting them I can skip to the good stuff or set a few extra goals to overcome the suffering…. But there's no entry into Christ's presence without the cross. No one has to go looking for one, the cross finds you." (David Goetz, *Death by Suburb*)

The cross finds us. The cross is different for each of us — a cross that fits our strength to carry it, and the service that we can give. A cross that uses our struggles and heartache to connect us to the hurt of the world. A cross that uses our sorrow, as much as our strength.

We can lament that we don't have the picture-perfect life, or we can turn and pick up the crosses in our lives. Pick up the cross of recovery… of the ill family member… of inclusion… of chemotherapy… of getting home in time for family time… of anger management… of trust. Pick up the cross of helping someone with no discernible benefit… of serving somewhere new… of talking to someone you don't agree with, and have nothing in common with, and move more deeply into faith.

That's the core of our faith. Taking up the cross, following the Jesus who loves and serves. That's our elevator speech. That's the essence of our faith.

That's what is on Jesus' business card and should be on ours, too.

The answer to the mystery of faith, and the entrance into it. Amen.

More Than A Bad Day?

The late Mike Yaconelli, who was a youth ministry guru and the pastor of a unique and small church, told a story about preaching at his church. He said that nearly every time he preached, a young woman named Maria raised her hand and asked, "Now, what exactly are you talking about?" After one sermon, Maria, who was about sixteen at the time, raised her hand, and this time she asked if she could pray for him. "Sure," he said. She asked if she could come up to the front, and he agreed. In the middle of the service, she walked up to the front, and her prayer was something like, "God, thank you for Mike. We all know that if he weren't in this church, we would all be lost, including him. Amen."

No doubt, in that church, as Maria was asking her questions, and coming up to the front, the congregation was wondering what in the world was going on. No doubt, in the temple, as Jesus was pouring out the coins and turning over the tables in the temple, his disciples had the same question. What is he up to now? Is he going to get us all in trouble? What is he trying to tell everyone? Or, as a teenager asked me once, "Is Jesus trying to say something, or is he just having a bad day?"

We know that Jesus knows the temple well. His parents faithfully bring him there after his birth, and he comes with family as a teenager for the Passover. The story says that this is customary for the family, so he may have been there other times, too. He spends enough time there to know the building, and where he can find the animals for sacrifices, and the people changing the money. He's seen all of this happening on the family visits to the temple. Perhaps his family talks about the financial burden of making the sacrifices, or they plan carefully so they can afford them, putting money away a little at a time.

Of our four gospels, Matthew, Mark, and Luke are strongly similar, but John always has a different take on things. Only a few stories make it into all four gospels, and this is one of them. Matthew, Mark, and Luke remember it happening near the end of Jesus' life, during his last week in Jerusalem, just before his death. They place it between Palm Sunday and Easter. There it serves as a final message.

But John remembers it at the beginning of Jesus' ministry. He places this moment in the temple between the story of Nicodemus coming to Jesus at night, and Jesus' meeting with the Samaritan woman at the well in the noonday heat. Both of those stories are about dismantling long-held ways of thinking, and Jesus is making that same point here. Adding to the layers of meaning, John writes this down after the physical temple has been destroyed. Writing to people who have always found God in the temple, John points us to another way of finding God.

We might have similar ideas about where to find God.

If we're life-long churchgoers, we connect God with the church. We hear God in the sound of the organ, feel the Spirit in the light of the stained glass windows, and breathe in the peculiar smell of church every week. It may even be a particular congregation, and a particular building, where we find God. All over the country, churches are doing less outreach work, and paying pastors less and less, so they can afford to stay in their buildings. When the choice is between a full-time pastor and a new roof, the roof wins. When there's a choice between a part-time pastor and a new boiler, the boiler trumps.

We understand the attachment to a beloved building, and a certain way of living out our religion.

Of all the churches I've served over the years, and the ones I've worked with through denominational committees, I have a secret favorite. I'll call them First Church of Possibility.

I met First Church when they were between pastors, and so I preached for them on some Sunday mornings. Their sanctuary was unusual. They had church on Sunday mornings in a rented building that was used for weddings on Saturdays, and meetings during the week. The coffee hour was bountiful but time-limited, since another church came to use the building in the afternoon. The building was new, the restrooms were spotless, and people who were walking by stopped in for church some Sundays. The members kept giving to the church, and they had very low expenses, so they had money to give away. They picked a community organization each month and gave generously to their work.

First Church ran into trouble with their landlord, and they needed a new home. I kept trying to fix First Church up with another congregation, like church blind dating. They had energy and money to devote to mission, but no building. Other churches had buildings with no people in them. It would seem like a match made in, ahem, heaven. For a time, First Church shared a building with another church. I'll call them Second Church of the Revered Past. After a while, the two groups got around to talking about merging together into one congregation. First Church was excited that they might have more partners to do mission work. They would make younger friends who could carry the energy of the church out into the world. Second Church was excited that First Church would bring them enough money to fix their leaky roof.

In the end, the DNA of the two congregations was too different for them to merge happily. First Church is now happily nesting with another congregation, now in their fourth location counting their original building, and still going strong. Sometimes the members drive by their first building, a magnificent structure with vaulted ceilings and Tiffany stained glass. They smile and keep driving, happy with where they are now.

The members of First Church know what we all have to learn. Much as we love the church building where we got married, where our kids were baptized, where the funerals of beloved people took place, God isn't tied down there. In fact, God may have already left the building, if all we do is talk about the roof and the water bill and the heating system. Just like the people around Jesus, we get tied down to a place, and think God belongs there.

Scholar Amy-Jill Levine, who has added greatly to my understanding of Jesus in his Jewish context, says that "recognizing Jesus within his Jewish context means recognizing his enormous concern for how people relate to each other on a day-to-day basis. The issue for him is not, "Here's what you need to believe in order to get into heaven." The issue is, "Here's what you need to do in order to have one foot in the kingdom of heaven. Here's what you need to do because here's what God wants you to do, and here's what your tradition calls you to do." It is his Judaism that associates love of God with love of neighbor; his Judaism emphasizes what we call the golden rule, also found in a number of different religious traditions. That's why he talks to people about reconciliation and says that human interaction is more important than ritual." (from an interview in the October 2012 issue of *US Catholic*)

God shows up where the people are: at the temple, or on the hillside; in the banquet hall or the upper room. God shows up in church sanctuaries, and also brew pubs and coffee shops, hospital chapels and labyrinths, office buildings and living rooms. God shows up where the relationships are. God shows up where our minds are open, and our hearts are ready.

May we be listening, and watching, this Lent.

In Jesus' name, Amen.

Embarrassing Visits

The lectionary reading for today gives us verses 14-21, but that's like reading the end of the mystery book without knowing the whole story. So, we have included all of the verses today.

John 3:1-21

Now there was a Pharisee named Nicodemus, a leader of the Jews. He came to Jesus by night and said to him, 'Rabbi, we know that you are a teacher who has come from God; for no one can do these signs that you do apart from the presence of God.' Jesus answered him, 'Very truly, I tell you, no one can see the kingdom of God without being born from above.' Nicodemus said to him, 'How can anyone be born after having grown old? Can one enter a second time into the mother's womb and be born?' Jesus answered, 'Very truly, I tell you, no one can enter the kingdom of God without being born of water and Spirit. What is born of the flesh is flesh, and what is born of the Spirit is spirit. Do not be astonished that I said to you, "You must be born from above." The wind blows where it chooses, and you hear the sound of it, but you do not know where it comes from or where it goes. So it is with everyone who is born of the Spirit.' Nicodemus said to him, 'How can these things be?' Jesus answered him, 'Are you a teacher of Israel, and yet you do not understand these things?

'Very truly, I tell you, we speak of what we know and testify to what we have seen; yet you do not receive our testimony. If I have told you about earthly things and you do not believe, how can you believe if

I tell you about heavenly things? No one has ascended into heaven except the one who descended from heaven, the Son of Man. And just as Moses lifted up the serpent in the wilderness, so must the Son of Man be lifted up, that whoever believes in him may have eternal life

'For God so loved the world that he gave his only Son, so that everyone who believes in him may not perish but may have eternal life.

'Indeed, God did not send the Son into the world to condemn the world, but in order that the world might be saved through him. Those who believe in him are not condemned; but those who do not believe are condemned already, because they have not believed in the name of the only Son of God. And this is the judgment, that the light has come into the world, and people loved darkness rather than light because their deeds were evil. For all who do evil hate the light and do not come to the light, so that their deeds may not be exposed. But those who do what is true come to the light, so that it may be clearly seen that their deeds have been done in God.'

For many years, I lived in a small town. It was fun to be able to walk to the community center, the hair salon, and the library. Since I could walk there, I went to the library a lot. I knew the staff, and it was easy to run in and get a new book. It was fun to talk to the staff, and catch up on their news whenever I went in.

But because I knew the library staff so well, there were certain things that I never, ever checked out there. If I had something embarrassing to check out, I went to the library in the next town over, where they didn't know me... and where I wouldn't run into my neighbors with a big stack of cringe-worthy books.

Remembering that, I have a lot of sympathy for Nicodemus, coming to see Jesus at night.

For us, Jesus is the big deal, but in their world, Nicodemus was the bigger figure. He was well-known as a Jewish leader, and it would have been embarrassing to be seen with Jesus… or to have people think he needed help with a religious question. If the Jewish leaders were upset with Jesus, he didn't want to be caught on the wrong side.

I wonder how any nights Nicodemus thought about coming to Jesus before he did? How many nights did he run through his questions in his mind? How many times did he start out, and then turn back around out of fear? And finally, he had to come. Something inside him won't let him rest… until he talked to Jesus.

That's what new birth in faith is like for most of us.

Some of you have a dramatic moment of faith when you were born anew into faith, or accepted Jesus into your heart. For others of us — myself included — being born anew into faith is a long walk with God. There are moments of God's presence that move us forward. And there are also lessons we learn slowly.

Nicodemus finally worked up the nerve to come to Jesus.

He started with a little flattery, and Jesus dropped him right into a discussion about God. By the end his head was spinning, and he probably had a big headache. He came to Jesus as a prominent religious figure, and Jesus told him he had to be born again. Well, he was just fine with the birth he had, thank you very much.

In his world, birth set your status in the world. People who study ancient Israel tell us, "the honor derived from one's status at birth, was simply a given. It usually stayed with a person for life.... To be born *over again*, born for a second time…" would change all of that. "Thus, a second birth, especially if it differed substantially in honor level from the first birth, would be a life-changing event of staggering proportions." (Bruce Malina and Richard kRohrbaugh in *Social-Science Commentary on the Gospel of John*)

It is unthinkable.

It's not that Nicodemus was slow to grasp this. With his questions, he was stalling for time. He had a lot to lose.

I have been Nicodemus a few times in my life.

When I go to a baby shower, and people ask everyone there for a piece of parenting advice, the thing I say is that you have to become a parent to the kid you actually get, instead of the one you planned on. But I see now that I didn't really take in the work of that until my daughter Lucy fell into a years-long battle with depression. It's her struggle, not mine, and she gave me permission to talk about it.

I thought I knew how to be a reasonably effective parent. You know: the balance of love and structure, the importance of family, nurturing the talents the child has. There were vegetables and books and math lessons in the summer… that was a big hit, as you can imagine.

When she stopped going to high school, when she had to be in the hospital, when we had to keep trying different medication until she found the right one, I had to learn to be a different kind of parent. I wasn't taking pictures at the prom… I was driving her to the hospital almost every day.

You have a similar challenge in your life.

Maybe it's learning to be born again into the reality of being divorced or having cancer. Maybe you're being born again into a new career, or into figuring out how to live life sober.

Glennon Doyle tells a story [in *Love Warrior*] about hitting a low point in her life as young woman. She had already been through a lot – an eating disorder at ten, drinking heavily by thirteen, and time in a hospital for her mental health by seventeen. She said she had a happy childhood, which added to her guilt about why she was such a mess. As she often tells on her blog and in her books, by college, she was a full blown alcoholic, grabbing a beer as soon as she got up, and taking it into the shower with her.

Feeling awful about herself, one night she stumbled into a Catholic church to make her confession to the priest. On the way to the confessional, she found a small room that was warm and safe, with the smell of incense and in that room she felt less alone. She tripped on the carpet and took off her shoes, letting her feet sink into the carpet. The softness was comforting. She saw a huge painting of Mary, cradling baby Jesus, with a tender, compassionate look on her face. She looked at Mary, and Mary looked at her, and she knew that, even though she was a mess, inside and out, Mary loved her.

Then the priest came in, and for a moment, she felt afraid. He seemed tired, exasperated by the depth of her problems. He folded his hands and listened to her. She shook in the bright lights, and because she was cold, and he looked at her like she was some kind of junkie. "Which I am," she said, "but right now I'm just cold." He told her she could be forgiven if she repented and said she was sorry.

In the small room, God felt like a mother to her. God is an administrator. She told the priest that she was sorry, and the priest let her go with a feeling of disdain. The disapproval was expected. The surprise, for her, was this feeling of acceptance and warmth from Mary.

She cried all the way home, not because the priest was indifferent, but because Mary saw the good in her. She thought, "I feel sad but real. Mary saw the good me trapped inside. That means the good me is real."

We all have to be born anew — born into our own goodness... a new world of faith... born into new ways of being church... born into connecting with people outside our walls. We have to be born into who God calls us to be, and into the life we have. And we are not alone in this. We are born from above — and the Holy Spirit, blowing where it wants to, is our partner in this.

Glennon Doyle said that moment in the church of her childhood, and the power of sitting with Mary, reminded her of a moment in her childhood. The ice cream truck came to her neighborhood, and while the man in the truck was selling popsicles out of the window, a teenager had broken into the back. He was handing them out for free out the back door, where the man couldn't see him. There was a short line at the window, and a long line for the free ones at the back.

The Holy Spirit is like the teenager handing things out. Not recommending theft, certainly, but the free gift. We just have to be ready to receive it.

The gospels don't tell us how, but Nicodemus got the gift. He appeared two more times in John's gospel. Most poignantly, when Jesus died, he came and prepared the body for burial. He had learned to the do the hard work. He had been born anew and joined to the light of Jesus.

May we be born and born again and again into life in God's Holy Spirit.

May we live with the joy of the Spirit, who sees the good, the real, the true within us, and helps us bring it to life in God's realm. May we be born again and again as God's people, always more deeply into faith.

In Jesus name, Amen.

Fifth Sunday in Lent

John 12:20-33

Seeing What We Don't Want To See

As we draw near to the end of Lent, how has your Lenten journey been? What spiritual practice did you add? What habit did you let go of to make room for God? I love hearing the variety of answers, such as reading a devotional each day, or dedicated time to read bigger chunks of the Bible. Maybe it is participating in a Lent Bible study or praying in a different way, just to try it out. Perhaps it is giving up a habit that distracts from God's presence — online games, shopping, or taking your phone to bed.

As we get near the end of Lent, these Greek travelers are really us. Everything we've been doing in Lent, all the small groups, the dinners, the weekly communion, the reading, the praying is meant to move us closer to what they're asking for. "We wish to see Jesus," said these strangers. That's our prayer, too, and the end of Lent sharpens our longing. Are we any closer than when we started, to seeing Jesus? Some of us are, I'm sure, and some of us are still hoping for a better look at him.

This story begins right after Jesus raises Lazarus from the dead. The crowd of people who see him bring life out of death can't stop talking about it, can't stop testifying. Word is spreading far and wide. Even these strangers have heard about it and came to see Jesus. The story calls them "Greeks," probably meaning Jews who lived outside the area and had come for the Passover. The Greeks came to Phillip and Andrew, who had the most Greek sounding names of the disciples, maybe hoping they would get the best reception from fellow countrymen.

But Jesus says no. He has never turned anyone away who came for help, that I can recall. But this time his mind was set on something ahead. He could have had a quick chat with the Greeks and moved on... but he was fixed on his purpose.

His answer here reminds me of the oft-used saying in business: "the good is the enemy of the great." There are lots of things we *could* do. We have so many choices. We could take up a bunch of hobbies, projects for work, or church plans. There are lots of things we could do easily, that wouldn't even take very much time. In a world where my attention is often scattered, I draw strength from Jesus' reminder to fix my attention on the main thing. God is calling all of us to do a few things well... but we get distracted by all the things we can do easily or quickly or because we like to do them. Jesus is fixed on one thing now — heading toward the cross.

He set the stage for his friends by telling them that they have to let go of their own lives. If you love your life, if you hold onto it tightly, if you care too much about it, you lose it. Curious.

That same message can be translated as life, soul, or spirit. It's whatever is at our center. If we love it too much, we'll end up losing it; if we hate it, and let it go, we have it forever. Jesus is speaking in Aramaic, which has a characteristic way of overstating things to make a point. As an old friend of mine used to say: "I exaggerate for clarity." Same with the way Jesus spoke. Hate your life, he told us. Strong stuff.

John's gospel is very clear that there is a conflict between the life of discipleship and the life of the world. It's hard to live in two worlds. Unless we become like seeds which are willing to die for a greater harvest, we will lose ourselves in chasing what we think we want. We let go of ourselves to find something greater.

But how in the world are we to do that? We're taught to hold onto things... save money, guard our health, work hard for success. We'll never get anything without hard work. You can't get far if you don't strive. All that advice is good for living in the world.

Jesus has a claim on our lives, our souls, and he's asking us to learn to let go. And it's not easy.

"My soul is troubled," Jesus said. We can feel his distress, the pain of this choice. If it's hard for him, then it's all the worse for us. The passage says "Unless a grain of wheat falls into the earth and dies, it remains just a single grain." (John 12:24) This same passage can be translated as "the grain of wheat remains alone."

The only way to learn this kind of sacrifice is with each other. Living with partners or children, taking care of an ill friend or a parent, committing ourselves to life in a community of faith, are the only ways I know to get out of our own selfishness. It is some kind of commitment to something outside us. Our souls rub up against the needs and wishes of someone else and are shaped in the process. Out of our commitment to a church or a person or a cause, we let go of what we want... and are made into better people. Every time we repeat something to a forgetful parent... run an errand for a sick friend... play a boring game with a toddler for the thirtieth time... listen to a friend tell a story we've heard before... we begin to let go of ourselves. Every time we let someone else have their way...support someone in their recovery... let a child make a choice, and develop their own independence... we set ourselves aside, and practice what Jesus is talking about.

People sometimes tell me that they can find God just as well sitting outside, on the golf course, or hiking a beautiful trail, as they can at church. Of course, finding God is not the issue. God is everywhere and always.

The issue is that we never learn to let go of ourselves and our selfishness in those places. We never become better people without other people. We never grow without other people to aggravate us, to mirror our own flaws, and show us where we're weak, and point out our silliness. We remain alone, if we don't have that in our life of faith. The God of the golf course and the hiking trail is always going to be a pale imitation of God, because that's all we can do for ourselves.

This is tough stuff. We would love to go back to the sweet Jesus who loves the little children, and doesn't ask too much of us, either. But Jesus insists that he's no simple, sweet, Wonder Bread® Jesus — he's the real deal, rough, and tough to swallow sometimes. But he is a redeemer who can stand up to tough times, stand up to the worst we can face, and be there with us. He can stand up to the evil of his own time, and the evil of ours.

When our hearts are broken, when we meet up with pain and suffering...when the world makes no sense... when we see injustice seem to triumph... then the simple, sweet, Wonder Bread® Jesus won't do. We need the Savior who knows how to suffer, as we suffer. We need the Jesus who understands sacrifice, and that it leads us toward God.

We are invited to be like the grain of wheat, part of something bigger, part of a life we can only glimpse on our own, until Jesus shows it to us. We need the redeemer who understands all about sacrifice and suffering, because we have to go down that road, too. And we are following him toward the cross, and toward Easter. If we see him, we can follow him, even to the end.

In Jesus' name, Amen.

Liturgy of the Palms

Mark 11:1-11

Text Message From Jesus

It was often said that the late President Reagan was the "great communicator." He was very talented, but the title really belongs to Jesus. In all the gospel stories that we have, he's always communicating something. Every time he heals someone, there's a message about God's love for people. Every time he teaches, there's a lesson about who God is, or who Jesus is, or who the people of God should be. Every time he pokes the religious authorities, there's a warning. Whenever he acts on the sabbath, there's a message. His actions always tell a story, and all the stories have been adding up to this day. We call it Palm Sunday, and it's the start of our holiest week, the week between today and Easter.

As we watch Jesus enter Jerusalem each year, we wonder what he's telling us.

The story is so intriguing that each of the four gospel writers remembered it and wrote it down. Our mental image of the day is a combination of all four but each one remembered different details. Mark's version doesn't have a single palm branch in sight, but we mentally add them in from other versions of the story. Mark's story, the one we hear today, is much simpler, but we also add in the crowds to our image of the day.

So what does Jesus want us to know?

Should we see Jesus as a king, as the descendant of Israel's great King David? Is he here to take up the throne? Is he the king entering this ancient city in triumph? Jesus goes to a lot of trouble to ride in on a colt — the sign of a ruler coming in peace. The first hearers of this gospel would have understood the reference to the prophet Zechariah, who promised, "Lo, your king comes to you, humble and riding on donkey." (Zechariah 9:9) The garments in the road are another gesture of welcome for a king.

Or should we understand Jesus as the long-awaited messiah? The cult has never had a rider because it is an animal used for a sacred purpose. This is the Passover season, the holiday which celebrates God setting the people free from slavery in Egypt. The messiah is the one to bring deliverance from the Romans — or so they think. Jesus comes into Jerusalem from the east, from the Mount of Olives, where Jewish tradition held that the messiah would come in the last days.

Or are we to look for another purpose? Noted preacher Fred Craddock called it a "protest march" (*Christian Century*, April 5, 2003) .This is the long culmination of Jesus' protests against the abuses he sees around him. All along, Jesus has disagreed with the common wisdom about who can eat at the table, who's included in God's kingdom, and what the sabbath means. Now, in the political and religious capital, he ratchets the protest up another notch.

He's using the symbols people understand to make a point they won't understand until later. He's showing them who he is, using the symbols of king and messiah to show that he is something different altogether.

Oh, and there's one more thing. Only Jesus knows that this is also a funeral procession.

What Jesus came to communicate was about the power of sacrifice.

He had come to reveal the power of bending our wills toward what God wants. It was the lifetime call to serve the least and the lost. It was the pattern of loving one another, even in the face of betrayal and fear.

Perhaps you've heard the story of the monastery that had begun to decline.

The monastery was once a grand place, with beautiful buildings, bustling with activity and prayer. Now there were only five monks left, and all of them were elderly and dispirited,

Nearby, in the woods, was a little hut where a rabbi from a nearby synagogue would come to pray. One day, it occurred to the abbot that he should go and seek the advice of the rabbi, his wise colleague. He knocked on the door, and the rabbi welcomed the abbot into the hut. When the abbot explained the purpose of his visit, the rabbi could only sympathize with him. "I know," he said. "I have the same problem. Almost no one comes to the synagogue anymore." The abbot and the rabbi talked and prayed together. When the abbot was leaving, he asked one more time. "Is there nothing you can tell me, no piece of advice you can give me?"

"I'm sorry," the rabbi told him. "I have no advice. I can only tell you that the Messiah is among you."

When the abbot got back to the monastery, the other monks gathered around him to ask what advice the rabbi had for them. He didn't have any suggestions, the abbot said sadly. All he said was something strange, the abbot reported. The Messiah is among us.

All the old monks thought about this as they did their work. Could there be any truth in what the rabbi had said? The Messiah is among us? They wondered if he could have meant one of them. In that case, which one? Could it be this one? No, he's too grumpy... but just in case, I'll treat him with respect. How about that one? No, too flighty... but just in case, I'll treat him with reverence. Or, what about this one of us? No, too young... but just in case, I'll treat him with honor. Or, each monk wondered, could it be me? Just in case, I'd better act with faith and honesty at all times, just in case.

As they thought about this, the old monks began to treat each other with great respect, just in case one of them was the Messiah. And on the off chance that each monk might himself be the Messiah, they began to act with honesty and compassion.

People still came to visit the monastery from time to time.

They would picnic on the lawn, to walk along the paths, or go into the run-down chapel to meditate. When they were there, even without realizing it, they felt the aura of extraordinary love that filled the place.

That spirit of generosity and faith was strangely attractive. People began to come back to the monastery more frequently to walk, picnic, to play, to pray. They began to bring their friends with them. And their friends brought their friends. Some people even asked the abbot about joining. After a few years, the monastery was again filled with people. Thanks to the rabbi's gift, it was a vibrant place of light and prayer.

What if we all lived as if the Messiah was among us?

Palm Sunday reminds us that the Messiah *is* among us. He invites us to live his brand of generosity and respect. He invites us read the signs, and take up his work of love.

Jesus is the king who rejects every kind of power, except the power of sacrifice. As a king, his only triumph is when we love another. He is the Messiah, coming in triumph to bring the age of God's rule - not winning the world by war, but as the prince of peace. Not by splitting the Mount of Olives in two and starting the final battle, but by winning the battle in our souls.

His new age begins when we, too, join in the battle to change the world. His life is only a success if we turn around everything we think we know and see through the eyes of the one riding on a colt, feet dragging in the dust, seeing with love the fickle hearts and frail faith of the crowd.

Sacrifice is the only path to power, and love is the only power that matters. The palms branches and the shouts are all a sign of God's love for us and the coming of God's new world. That's what Jesus is trying to tell us.

Jesus ends the story all alone, but he's still communicating with us.

If we understand, we can follow him into this week of mystery, and beyond.

We can read the signs, and join his kingdom, this week, and always. Amen.

Liturgy of the Passion

Mark 14:1-15:47

Never Really Alone

Kate Bowler is a professor who studies the Prosperity Gospel — the idea that God rewards us with cars and money and big houses, if we love God enough. Anything good in your life is a reward from God, so the idea goes, because you are especially worthy. The idea falls apart when you look at the reverse — all the faithful, hard-working, committed people who love God deeply... and don't live in big houses or; have millions in the bank.

If God actually worked that way, pre-school teachers would drive Maseratis, and nurses would collect fine art. All of you would be millionaires, and football players and movie stars would live in small apartments.

We all know it doesn't work that way.

When she was diagnosed with cancer, Kate Bowler had to rethink all of these ideas. Her diagnosis has caused her to think hard about some things. She wrote, [on her blog] "Most of my worst thoughts hover around a single word. **Alone.**"

The experience of being ill is so lonely, so isolating, that she felt like she was all alone in that. You may feel that way in your own illness, or when you're struggling financially, or when a loved one is in prison. You may feel that way when you have a failure in life, or when things aren't going the way you planned. You may feel that way when you're carrying a secret that no one can understand, or when you're afraid of people judging you.

As Jesus comes into what we now call Holy Week, the last week of his life, he is profoundly, deeply alone.

As we picture Palm Sunday, we know that it's also Passion Sunday, the Sunday that leads to Jesus' death.

How do you imagine Jesus' friends and followers, welcoming him into Jerusalem? How do you picture the crowd in your mind? One thing I never thought about until recently was the expression on Jesus' face. A Lent book I love suggests, "Surely few of us picture [Jesus as] stern and stoic, ignoring the joy all around him, or anxious and jittery, waiting for the other shoe to drop, or rolling His eyes in dismissal of the nonsense. I picture Jesus smiling, looking around him at the radiant faces of the twelve and the hope-filled eyes of the masses. Knowing that the twelve would soon run for their lives and the masses would soon reject him, Jesus still stayed fully present for the party." (Alicia Britt Chole, *Forty Days of Decrease*)

Jesus knows that he's soon to be betrayed and rejected. He alone can see ahead to the end of the story. But there's this one moment of joy, as Jesus fulfills the ancient prophecies about the messiah. There's such joy in the crowd that we still celebrate it all these centuries later.

Only Jesus knows that this is also a funeral procession.

Hailed as a king at the start of the week, Jesus ends it under a mocking sign: the king of the Jews. The entrance into the city and using symbols of the king and the conqueror will lead to his death before the week is over.

He alone knows that he's not that kind of Messiah, not the conquering hero the crowd is looking for, not planning to overthrow the Romans and the corrupt religious leaders.

But there is one person who sees him as he is.

Jesus takes time in this last week to have dinner at the house of a friend. The story calls him Simon the Leper. Even if Simon was healed by Jesus, he's still known by his former illness. This woman comes in with her nard — a very expensive ointment. It was so expensive that it was often a family heirloom, something passed down from parent to child to grandchild because it was too good to be used. The right occasion never came up. You have those dishes, right, that you never use? Or that outfit that's waiting for a special occasion? Or that special bottle of something you're saving?

People used these alabaster jars to store this expensive ointment. It was imported from India, and the jar was sealed to keep the ointment from drying up, and you had to break it to use it.

The story says that "they" scolded her.

We don't know if "they" are the disciples, or the other guests. There's plenty to criticize here, if anyone wants to. She's butting into a dinner party. She's touching a man who's not related to her. But the complaint seems to be about the money. This is an extraordinary act of love and devotion. The complainers, too, don't see what this woman sees.

Like Jesus, she, too, is alone in what she sees.

There are times when we have this same feeling of being alone.

Kate Bowler, says, writing about being alone in her cancer journey: "I am locked inside this body, which is failing me. And it keeps me from breaking through, back to the life I want." Still, in that loneliness, there is a cure. She hears small whispers in her spirit which tell her: *"you are loved, you are loved, you are loved."* She can feel God in moments when God seems to announce to her that God is present. She recalls, "The most alone I have ever been is when I woke up from my surgery. The room was empty and all I could hear was the chirping of the heartrate monitor. The hospital had, of course, taken everything that was familiar to me. My dress I love to teach in. My ring from the man I love. All I had was my hospital gown and a carved up body I hardly recognized. And then I saw it. Something around my wrist. It was a bracelet. But not just any bracelet. It was a slap bracelet, the kind I played with when I was ten and they were all the rage. It was such an absurd situation, the more I thought about it. Someone had crept into my room, past security, and quietly slapped it on my wrist so I would have it when I woke up. It was bright neon. It was hideous. And all it said was: FIERCE."

We are never as alone as we think we are.

Jesus, alone in the crowd, meets up with the woman who gives him a tender gift. In the crowd, everyone sees him as he is not — king, conqueror, hero. She sees him as he is and sees his coming death. He sees her for who she is, too.

This week, as we come into Holy Week, may we see Jesus as he is, and keep him company in this journey of suffering. And may he go with us, in every place where we feel abandoned, lost, fearful, doubting… so we know that we are never alone. Amen.

John 13:1-17, 31b-35

Feet And Hearts

A generation or two after Jesus' life, when the gospel writers wrote down all their memories, the writers recalled this night differently. John remembered Jesus washing the disciples' feet — a sign of being a servant to them, a nudge to help them serve others. Matthew, as well as Mark and Luke, all remembered a meal.

Both can be true in the heart sense of true, because they call to mind the same thing — Jesus is saying farewell to the people who have been so close to him and giving them a way to remember him. Both memories are all about the things we can see and hold, about the simplest things that get filled with the power of Jesus.

We know that we remember the important things.

Things like what you had for lunch last week, and where you parked the car two weeks ago are probably gone from your mind. We don't need to know them anymore, and so our brains give us a break and sweep them away.

Other things we're desperate to remember.

The sound of a loved one's voice, after they die. The way they smell, once we lose their physical presence. How small a brand new baby is, and what the baby feels like in our hands. We hold onto cell phone messages and old shirts so we can remember. We keep trying to remember, for memory is a big part of who we are. And, when we can't remember anymore, other people remember for us.

This night Jesus gives us ways to remember him. He's present with us all the time, of course, but being creatures who live in the tangible world, we need something to hold onto. And so we have this table — the place where Jesus meets us in the bread and cup, and we remember his giving himself for us that we might share in his life. And so we have him washing his friends' feet, and our chance to wash each other's hands tonight, so we can remember what it is to serve, to love one another fully.

This night also reminds us of the depths of human emotion. Tonight and tomorrow, we see the worst that people can do. Tomorrow isn't surprising — we can understand why the authorities want to kill Jesus, why he can't live any longer, challenging them, turning over tables in the temple, saying because of Jesus their faith is meaningless. We can see why the Romans are worried about an uprising.

But tonight…

…these are the people closest to Jesus. He's been telling them for a while now that his death is near. He knows it, and they must know it, too. When people are in crisis, they do more of what they usually do to cope. People who drink, drink more, people who eat, eat more, talkers talk more and more loudly, worriers worry more. It must have been a stressful room to be in, that upper room. These are the people closest to Jesus, and they don't do any better by him than strangers will tomorrow. This must have been the betrayal that stung the most.

In this night, we see in the disciples what we know is in ourselves… the depth of our fears… our vanity… our need to control the outcome of things… the depth of our doubt… our fickleness of faith when things don't go well… our inattention… our small thinking.

Jesus sees all of that in his friends, as he sees it in us, and what does he do?

He comes closer.

He doesn't throw up his hands and give up.

He doesn't run away.

He comes closer.

On this night, he gives his friends — and us — these enduring signs of his presence. In the depths of human emotion, in the worst that we can be, at our least faithful, he comes closer. Everyone is welcome at the table. Everyone is blessed with a final touch of his hands, a final gift of service. No one is left out.

When we come to the communion table tonight, we take this memory into our hands so we can feel and taste the presence of Jesus. Right here.

In this night of shadows, may we remember together the dimness that lives in us and in all humanity... and also that we follow a Savior who, in times of pain and emptiness, is there, too.

At the basin, at the table, in our memory, we find him with us.

There he is, coming closer. Amen.

Good Friday

John 18:1-19:42

Nothing Special Friday

If you were out at work this morning, or running errands, you know that most of the world is having a typical day today. People are going to the bank, to exercise, to shop for groceries. People are going to work and coming home. They are getting coffee, standing in line for a bagel, and chopping food for dinner. They're typing away, writing emails, developing code, designing buildings. Other people are giving or receiving medical tests, taking chemo and radiation, sitting through the hours of dialysis.

All over, there's nothing special about today.

And, it turns out, there's nothing special about Jesus, either.

We're here today because it's not quite enough to wave our palms and then bask in Easter's joy — we want to stand with Jesus' friends and family at the cross, watching and waiting. We, too, want to see where they put him, where his body ends up. There's something special about him to us… but not to anyone else.

The gospel writers spent as much time on Jesus' last few days as they did on everything else put together. Out of Mark's sixteen chapters, six are about the last week of Jesus' life. These memories must have stayed with Jesus' friends in sharp detail, and we get them in the same painful detail.

There's nothing special about Jesus — crucifixion was a common form of death. The words "cross" and "crucify" come from the generic Latin word for torture. This kind of death was so common that the vertical poles stayed in place — usually at the top of a hill, or by a well-traveled road, or at the city gate. The more people who saw the posts, the better. Maybe they'd be deterred from any rebellion against the ruling authorities. Prisoners commonly carried their own horizontal cross pieces, laboring under the weight of the wood so their fear could grow. It was common to flog people — to whip them, like Jesus is, to weaken the prisoner as much as possible.

For Jesus, there was one special incentive. The people doing the crucifixion were in a hurry. Jesus had to be dead and buried before sundown, to comply with the religious law.

Some people were nailed in place, and others tied in place. The placard that Jesus got was also common — passers-by could look and see what the criminal had done. "The King of the Jews" was a title that the Romans used for Herod. The title makes fun of Herod, the ruler of a small province, very far from all the important business of Rome.

They used it again to make fun of Jesus.

There was nothing special in the title.

There was not even anything special about the way the soldiers mocked Jesus.

I had always thought that the soldiers devised this punishment just for Jesus, mocking him as the king of the Jews, but it was part of the formula. Victims of crucifixion were mocked before and during the process. It was common to dress a prisoner up, and then make fun of him. The purple cloak was already hanging in the guardroom, long before Jesus arrived, and it hung there after he left, waiting for other prisoners.

For Jesus, they took it a step further. The purple cloak mocked the claim of royalty, and the crown of thorns was meant to evoke the laurel wreath that Caesar wore. The reed was a substitute for the rulers' scepter. These, too, were common for political prisoners.

Even dividing up the clothes of the person on the cross was common — a little overtime pay came for the soldiers who had to do this work.

There was not anything special about Jesus' burial, either.

The story says that:

The Burial of Jesus

When evening had come, and since it was the day of Preparation, *that is, the day before the sabbath, Joseph of Arimathea, a respected member of the council ...went boldly to Pilate and asked for the body of Jesus. Pilate allows him to take the body. A*nd then, as the gospel tells it, *"Joseph bought a linen cloth, and taking down the body, wrapped it in the linen cloth, and laid it in a tomb that had been hewn out of the rock. He then rolled a stone against the door of the tomb. Mary Magdalene and Mary the mother of Jesus saw where the body was laid."* (John 19:42-47)

Jesus' family and friends had to know where he was buried so they would know where to mourn. It was common for people to grieve at the entrance to the tomb — some tombs from that era have a shallow depression at the entryway so people could gather there and weep together. Nothing special about that, either.

There's not anything special about our suffering either.

There is plenty of it to go around.

Each of you has something going on in your life that's causing you pain. It could be an illness and painful treatment. Or, perhaps you're grieving for a loved one. Maybe your home isn't a safe place for you or your family is angry and divided. For some people here, there are more bills than money, and stress is eating away at you. For others, God seems far away.

Whatever it is, you're in good company.

All around us, other people are suffering in mental hospitals and prisons ...somewhere, someone is being tortured for their beliefs ...a young person is being bullied, and feeling their spirit wither ...a frazzled parent is hitting a child in anger ...a migrant worker is feeling an ache in their back, and it's just the start of the day. There's nothing special about any of that.

There's nothing special about any of it...

...except that the redeemer chose to enter into that suffering, and to fill it with the presence of God. He chose to bring the presence of God to every place of hurt, pain, and unbearable sorrow. He chose to make sure we know that God is never absent from the world, even when it doesn't make sense to us.

That's why today is special.

The Roman soldier saw it at the cross, and now we do, too.

At the very last, as Jesus gave up his spirit, the sound was so explosive, so clear that this was the breath of God, that the soldier looked up and said, "Truly this man *was* the Son of God." (Mark 15:39)

That same breath that went out of Jesus now fills up all of human life. It enters into every place of pain, sorrow, and anguish, and lets us know that God is there, too.

> *When you go out of church this afternoon,*
> *and to the grocery store,*
> *or the bakery,*
> *or the gym,*
> *you may feel a little dazed.*
> *As you zip to the bank,*
> *or finish your taxes,*
> *or call a friend on the phone,*
> *you may feel jarred, between the busy-ness of the world,*
> *and the business of standing watch at the cross.*

Things go on, and there's nothing special about today …except that we carry with us the cry of the Roman soldier, that truly this was the Son of God. We carry it now in our lives, bearing watch through the weekend, until Sunday comes.

In the name of the Son of God,

breath of life,

one acquainted with sorrows, Amen.

Going Where Jesus Goes

Mark's Easter story is missing something.

I never noticed it before because the tomb was there… the women followers of Jesus were there, ready to honor his body. After Jesus' death, they followed the body to see where it was buried. They waited, anxiously, until the sabbath was over, and then hurried to honor Jesus in death, and to grieve for him. We heard them fret about huge the stone in front of the grave and wonder if they can find someone to help them roll it away. The mysterious figure was there to give the news.

Then before this version — in Mark's version of the story — there's no Jesus.

In fact, the messenger says: "He is not here."

Um, this is Easter — if he's not here, where is he?

The women didn't wait around to ask too many questions. They rushed off, as the story says, seized by "terror and amazement." In the original Greek, the words are even sharper — trauma, and ecstasy.

The story ends in silence.

This ending is so unsettling that at last three different attempts have been made to fix it. It doesn't seem quite right to leave the story there, and later writes have added to the end.

Mark wrote this gospel down about forty years after the death of Jesus, in a time of upheaval for the Jewish people. The great temple was reduced to rubble. The people of Israel had rebelled against the Romans and sustained terrible losses. The followers of Jesus were separating from other Jews who didn't believe he was the Messiah. There's more and more distance between Jews who follow Jesus and Jews who are still waiting for the Messiah. These two groups with the same roots, sometimes even members of the same family, were dividing. Mark wrote his gospel into a world of terror. The bleakness of the ending matched the harshness of the times.

The women's reaction made perfect sense. They were seeing something they had never seen before. The first day of college, being the new kid at school, first day in the military, first date, the first time they let you take a baby home from the hospital and seem to think you can take care of it — we've all known the terror of something completely brand new.

We take the resurrection for granted because we know the story, but it's a huge surprise on that first day. I don't know that I would have been any different. In fact, I admire their courage. If you were expecting a body and you got a message that Jesus who was missing, being afraid makes perfect sense.

Still, we want more.

Like the women at the tomb, we want to know where Jesus is, and what he's up to.

Glennon Doyle wrote on her blog about teaching Sunday school at her church. The kids came into the sanctuary and sat down, listening to the teacher. After a bit, one little boy got restless and whispered to her: *"Excuse me. Is God coming?"* As she said, he looked around "like he was expecting God to show up here like Ronald shows up occasionally at McDonalds." (Momastery.com)

"Excuse me. Is God coming?"

That's the question, isn't it - when we look into the tomb and find it empty but we don't know what's coming next.

When the job ends.

When the divorce papers come in the mail.

When you're about to lose your house.

When the doctor comes in, and she isn't smiling.

When your child is lost to drugs.

When violence comes into your life and shakes your sense of safety.

Is God coming?

Mark wrote his gospel for people who were already believers.

They already knew the rest of the story.

They knew that God was coming, that God has come and is still coming.

The story is not so much about the empty tomb and the missing Jesus, but the reality that he's already at work again. He's already in Galilee, where they're all from, where it all began. He's not in any place that can contain him, seal him up, or keep him in place. He's in Galilee, where there's work to be done. The very first thing Mark ever says about Jesus is, "In those days Jesus came from Nazareth of Galilee and was baptized by John in the Jordan." (Mark 1:9)

He went back to where the work was.

He went to Galilee, and Chicago, and Syria.

He has gone to refugee camps, where parents are burying children today.

He has gone to the seat on the bus where someone is being bullied, and to the dark walkway where a woman is being harassed.

He's gone to the park bench where someone will try to sleep tonight, and to the empty dining room where a family is sitting without food.

He's gone ahead to the person standing on the edge of a bridge, planning to end their own life.

He's gone because he's busy, coming to us.

We can stand, peering into the tomb, wanting more.

We can get lost in our fear, or our surprise at something new.

Or, we can get up and go to Galilee, wherever we find it in our world, right now, and try to find the Jesus who can't be limited, can't be contained, and can't be held down by death.

We can go and find him, for he carries the good news with him. God is coming — to you and me and every place of terror and need, every place of pain and suffering, and every place of joy too.

He has good news for us and work for us to do alongside him.

He is not here — he has been raised.

Let's hurry and catch up with him.

In the name of the risen Christ, Amen.

Growing Into Our Scars

There's something about a scar that begs for a story.

When I see someone with an intriguing scar, I always want to know how they got it. It would be rude to ask, and so I don't, but I keep hoping it will come up in conversation. I wonder what lesson is behind the stitches on the knee …what adventure brought the scar on the forehead …what happened right before the mark on the arm? Sometimes it's a story of challenge and triumph. Other times it's a painful reminder of a past hurt. But there's always a story.

It intrigues me that, after his resurrection, Jesus could have come back without his scars, but he kept them. He could have appeared to his friends in his pre-death state, whole and shining with glory, but he chose to stay scarred. He picked this way of coming to the people he loves.

The people who wrote down the gospel stories could have skipped the ugly parts, too. They could have left out these stories of fear and doubt but they give us the whole picture, good and doubtful.

After the fear of the past week, after watching their beloved teacher die, the disciples had their own scars. The story says that the disciples were hiding in fear of the people who put Jesus to death, which is understandable. Would the authorities come looking for them next?

They may also have been hiding in fear of Jesus.

They had good reason to hide. They fell asleep when he needed them, they denied him, deserted him at the cross, and then gave in to fear.

But still Jesus came and what he said was: "Peace be with you." Don't fret, he was saying. Don't get stuck in the past.

The one with the scars is also the one with the ability to heal.

Thomas spoke to us about doubt, which we all have, but also about the power of not giving up. He missed the big reveal when Jesus came the first time. Instead of saying "oh well," and moving on, Thomas asked for what the other disciples got. He wanted to see for himself.

For the disciples, Jesus' death was a kind of death for them, too. They had to finally accept that Jesus wasn't exactly the Messiah they expected. This is a theme all through the gospels, but his death made it real. This was no conquering hero Messiah …not a war leader …this was the kind of teacher who reveals grace with his scars, not his perfection. This is the kind of teacher who is about service, not triumph.

We have this moment all the time, when we buckle down to the real job we have, instead of waiting for the perfect one …or make our peace with the real person we married, instead of the Hallmark card version of love… when we go to the college we can afford, instead of the one that looked so perfect on the tour …when we decide to show up for our real lives, instead of waiting until we have money, get braces, lose fifteen pounds, move into our dream house, and so on.

Thomas was ready — he was ready to see the scarred Jesus, instead of the perfect one. And he invites us to jump into our own imperfect, broken, battered lives in the same way.

Rachel Macy Stafford told a story about a teaching job and one of her own greatest teachers. He was, as she said "a 10-year-old boy born to a drug-addicted mother, with an Individualized Education Plan thicker than an encyclopedia — a boy with permanent scars along the side of his left arm from a beating with an extension cord when he was three."

She had a teaching job far from home, in a classroom full of children with deep needs. They were delayed in their learning, and difficult in their behavior. The first few months of school were hard, with tears on the way to work and tears on the way home. She prayed every day that this would be the day to make a difference for a kid.

"On this particular morning," she said, "I was excited. The other lead teacher and I had spent weeks teaching the children appropriate behavior for public outings. We would be going putt-putting and out to lunch. Miraculously, most of the children in class had earned this privilege — only a few had not."

Kyle was one of the students who had not earned the field trip, and he was angry. To show it, "he began screaming, cursing, spitting, and swinging at anything within striking distance. [And then] he did what he'd done at all his other schools, at home, even once at a juvenile detention center …he ran" right out into the traffic in front of the school.

And she ran after him. Kyle was fast. His older brothers were track stars at the high school. Fortunately, she had on tennis shoes for the field trip.

"Kyle took a sharp left and began walking through a dilapidated strip mall. [Getting tired,] he bent over with his hands on his knees, [trying] to catch his breath. That is when he saw me. I must have looked ridiculous — the front of my lightweight blouse soaked with sweat, my once-styled hair now plastered to the side of my beet red face. He stood up abruptly …but it was not a look of fear. I saw his body relax. He did not attempt to run again …My exhaustion caused me to slow to a walk. He opened his mouth to speak when a police car pulled up, abruptly filling the space between Kyle and me. The principal of the school and an officer got out. They spoke calmly to Kyle who [got into the car.]… Kyle eventually came back to school…. As weeks passed, he was glued to my side, complying with instructions, attempting to do his work, and once in a while even smiling. For a child with severe attachment issues, it was quite amazing that he was developing a bond with me. One day on the way to art class, Kyle unexpectedly grasped my hand. It was unusual for a boy his age and size to hold his teacher's hand, but I knew I must act like it was the most normal thing in the world.

I simply relished the moment — an unimaginable breakthrough from the child whose file bore the words: "Unable to express love or maintain a loving relationship with another human being." She adds, "Ten years have passed since I've seen Kyle… I see Kyle's face and remember I don't always have to have the answer. Because sometimes there is no clear-cut answer. I think of Kyle and remember the power of presence."

When Kyle ran away, the teacher told the speech therapist, who knew him well, how she felt like she had failed him. She said that she should have known how to do more for him. The therapist put her hand on the teacher's shoulder and told her what had made the difference. "No one ever ran after him before. No one. They just let him go."

The people with the scars turn into our teachers.

Our own scars also become our wisdom.

Our imperfection is also the gift we have to give.

Our bumps, bruises, and hurts are places where grace shows up. I should add that I mean this in a spiritual sense. If someone in your life is giving you real bumps and bruises, that's not God's will for any of us.

We think we make it through life in spite of our scars, but maybe it's because of scars. We think we have faith in spite of our doubts, and it turns out to be because of doubts. Grace shows up in the broken places. Glory shows up with the scars.

This is our story, the story of our own scars.

In the name of the risen and scarred Christ, Amen.

The Body Of Christ, On Repeat

Repetition is the key to success.

Whether it's learning a new soccer move, or a tennis swing, memorizing a poem, or learning a new language, we have to do it over and over again. We have to get the golf swing or the yoga move into our muscle memory. We have to learn just the right touch for sanding wood or kneading bread dough. We have to remember how to edit a video or play a song. It works with music, manners and art.

Repetition is part of building faith, too.

In this Easter season, one sighting of the resurrected Jesus isn't enough.

One conversation between him and the disciples won't work.

He kept showing up and showing up so the disciples could — and we can really understand this new reality. It takes a while for this to sink in.

Luke's gospel story finds us on Sunday evening, the day of resurrection, with Jesus busy continuing to make appearances to the people he loves. All four gospels have appearances outside the now-empty tomb, and then Jesus moved out into the wider world. Matthew and Mark remember these appearances happening in the Galilee, where the story began, but Luke left the disciples in Jerusalem. He left them fearful, hiding, and locked in, but still where it all happened.

Our faith is all about the tangible, the real, and what we can see and hold onto. That comes from Jesus himself, the giver of bread and cup, the hands-on healer, the foot washer. He went to a lot of trouble to show up in person, after his resurrection. He wanted his friends to know, without a doubt that he was real and alive in the physical body.

The stories go out of their way to tell us that this was not a ghost or a hallucination. The body of Christ is central to the stories — to Thomas believing when he touched Jesus, to the others who needed to feel and see him, even Jesus eating the fish to show us how real he was.

That particular body of Christ is gone, but there is a body of Christ still in the world. We — the church, community of faith, the people gathered now in Jesus' name — are the enduring body of Christ. These stories have something to tell us, the church, the living body of Christ, about our life of faith.

The body of Christ is persistent.

Jesus kept showing up to show his friends this new truth. One appearance wouldn't do it. This is the second story set on Easter night in Luke, and the other gospels have other stories. Until the job is done and the good news revealed, the living body of Christ keeps showing up.

The body of Christ meets needs.

The people who need to see Jesus to make it all real get that. Once, when I served as a hospice chaplain, a young man was extremely distraught about the upcoming death of his mother. Wanting to find something to hold onto, he asked me if he would see his mother again. He wondered if she would come to him in a dream or if he would feel her presence. I was stumped for a minute. I couldn't guarantee anything to him, and I didn't want to leave him with nothing. Running over past experiences in my mind, it struck me that there was a pattern.

In my experience, I said, each of us gets what we need. Whatever assurances people need will come to them, somehow. If you need that, I told him, you'll receive it. The same happened when Jesus showed up. The people who needed a reminder about the scriptures, and Jesus' part in God's plan, got that. The people who need a second chance got that. The people who needed to touch him get that. How many times, in the gospel of John, did Jesus tell Peter to feed his sheep? Three, as if to redeem each denial. Peter needed healing, and he got that.

The body of Christ points outside itself.

Jesus came with work to do for his friends. He was going to give them a share in God's power and he sent them out with a task. They were not meant to sit around reminiscing, but to go out and share what they knew. The body of Christ, looking outside itself.

The body of Christ resists locked doors.

Like those disciples, we, too, lock ourselves away. We close up part of our lives, forget to take chances, see people with suspicion, and think nothing better is possible. We close off places inside us or lock away our future plans. If we can just seal things up tightly enough, maybe we can fend off any future disasters and more grief, plus any other big pain.

As a congregation, we can lock our spiritual doors too, if our vision is too small… our prayers too limited… our hope too tiny. We forget that Jesus is the one who opens doors.

Just like some people can't resist a challenge, Jesus can't resist a closed-up place, something walled off, or a locked door. That's the place where he loves to come in and ask us what he asked those first disciples: "Why are you so afraid?"

In that way, the body of Christ is an antidote to fear. When we feel afraid, anxious, worried, out of strength, the body of Christ is medicine for that. "Be not afraid," Jesus says over and over in his ministry, and the risen Christ says it again here. "Peace be with you," is not just a greeting, it's a remedy for fear. "Peace be with you," we say, and we can catch encouragement and hope and strength from each other for this work of being the body of Christ in the world. What we can't do alone, we can do together — as a body of faith.

We may be wounded and frightened, scarred and scared, trying to lock ourselves away from pain and fear, and yet we are also called to resurrection living. We have been touched by the body of Christ, and now it's our turn to be that living body in the world.

We are the only body of Christ there is in this world, and God has work for us to do. "Peace be with you." Amen.

The Shepherd Knows

In this Easter season, the scripture texts take us back to the words of Jesus, words that the disciples recalled as they pondered the mystery of the resurrection, and what Jesus wanted them to do next.

Here Jesus speaks about himself as the shepherd, the guide and guard of those who love him.

John 10:11-18

'I am the good shepherd. The good shepherd lays down his life for the sheep. The hired hand, who is not the shepherd and does not own the sheep, sees the wolf coming and leaves the sheep and runs away — and the wolf snatches them and scatters them. The hired hand runs away because a hired hand does not care for the sheep. I am the good shepherd. I know my own and my own know me, just as the Father knows me and I know the Father. And I lay down my life for the sheep. I have other sheep that do not belong to this fold. I must bring them also, and they will listen to my voice. So there will be one flock, one shepherd. For this reason the Father loves me, because I lay down my life in order to take it up again. No one takes it from me, but I lay it down of my own accord. I have power to lay it down, and I have power to take it up again. I have received this command from my Father.'

I'm a city person. Too much open space makes me nervous, so when I started thinking about sheep, I had to call my brother, who lives on a farm in Wisconsin. I asked him what he knows about sheep, and the first thing he said was: "Sheep are stupid."

"Hmmm," I thought. All over the Bible, the people of God are compared to sheep. The familiar and beloved words of Psalm 23 proclaim right away that God is our shepherd, making us, by definition, sheep. Psalm 100 proclaims that we are the sheep of God's pasture, the flock of God's hand.

Every place we look, the biblical writers find comfort in the fact that God is our shepherd, and we shall not lack anything. Every need is met and every danger taken care of. There were plenty of dangers for shepherds in ancient Palestine. In that world, the shepherd was absolutely responsible for the lives of the sheep. Fighting off bears and wolves, along with thieves, was part of the job description. If an animal were eaten by a wolf or bear, the shepherd had to bring in part of the sheep's body to prove that the animal had eaten it.

The shepherd's staff mentioned in Psalm 23 is a weapon for such battles. The rod used there is the shepherd's crook, used to rescue lost lambs and guide the others over rocky hills. I love that the "rod" mentioned in "spare the rod, spoil the child" is the same Hebrew word as the shepherd's crook. Sparing the rod isn't about punishment — it's about guiding and helping, like the shepherd does with his crook.

In ancient Palestine sheep roamed without fences or strict boundary lines, and shepherds spent their days wandering with the sheep. They walked along as the sheep grazed, and at night they slept with the sheep. In the passage before this one, Jesus proclaimed that he was the gate. Sheep often slept in open enclosures, and the shepherd slept at the opening, to guard the sheep. With the shepherd there, the door is safe.

All along the way, the shepherd got to know the flock, and often gave each sheep a name. The shepherd knew which sheep was fearful and which one was likely to wander off, which one was irritable and which one was sweet.

In the Christian scriptures, the New Testament, Jesus picked up this same idea. And when Jesus proclaimed that, as the good shepherd, he knew his flock and they knew him, he was doing no more than any other shepherd.

But Jesus called himself not just a shepherd, but the *good* shepherd.

The Greek word translated as "good" is the strongest possible word for good — not the ordinary everyday word. It really means noble, beautiful, worthy, and exemplary. Jesus was telling his flock that he was the best possible shepherd — the ideal shepherd, one willing to lay down his life for the sheep. The shepherd beyond all others — the great shepherd.

In all of these "I am" sayings from John's gospel, Jesus compared himself with the most ordinary things — light, bread, water, and in this passage, a shepherd. He never said that he's the good king, or the new high priest, or the scholar who knew the truth. And, when he chose a shepherd, he chose a lowly, smelly job. He chose a job done by the children of the family or a hired hand.

It's true that at that time, "shepherd" was a frequent metaphor for the ruler of a country …but no one actually wanted to be a shepherd. Jesus was turning the image of the king on its head — using the metaphor but reminding his friends that he was the shepherd who knew the sheep, who lived with the sheep, who provided for the sheep. Seeing his friends, knowing their need for guidance and protection, he offered them the ancient image of the shepherd.

In our world, we don't see a lot of shepherds, but the image still tells us what kind of God we have. Maybe you're a city person, too, and the only sheep we see at are petting zoos and at a distance on road trips.

But we know enough to know that the shepherd can't lead the sheep anywhere, really, can't cajole them, yell at them, or expect them to follow. There is no planning ahead with sheep. The shepherd only gets anything done by being with the sheep — in the middle of the flock. In this, we understand something about our God. God insists on being in the middle of us, mixed into our lives, right in the midst of our stupid choices, our confusion, our tendency to wander off where we shouldn't be and our constant need to be called back.

I once preached on this text with a high-school-aged friend, and I loved what she said so much that she gave me permission to quote her. Now a graduate student, Megan said:

"This passage exemplifies Jesus' relationship with God and his relationship with us. Jesus says that he "knows his own sheep, and his

own sheep know him." However, as Christians this is what we strive to do our whole life. Jesus confidently says "the sheep will recognize my voice." Jesus is crazy! I am always looking for his word and guidance in my life... and I'm sure that most of the time I fail to see it. It is hard to distinguish what he is telling us from everything else we hear. I am not like the sheep in this passage. It is so easy for them to hear Jesus because there are no outside influences pulling them astray. For us the media is telling us how we should look, how we should dress, what we should buy. School and jobs influence how we spend our money. Our friends influence our choices."

She helped me understand how hard it is to hear the voice of Jesus, and how hard we have to work to listen.

There are plenty of dangers for us, too.

The danger of being seduced by our stuff or thinking that we're worth no more and no less than our title or salary, or forgetting the things that feed the soul, or living with our addiction, or being too busy. Our preoccupations with work, our screens, shopping, or easy anger lead us away from Jesus. We're constantly getting off the path and needing to be called back.

But, Megan said in that same sermon: "Nonetheless, Jesus is confident we will be able to distinguish him from all the other influences. The fact that Jesus is so sure we will be able to do it gives me hope. If Jesus is certain I will hear his voice, who am I to say I won't. As sheep we are all important to him. Jesus has told us it is possible to know him and it is possible to have a relationship with him."

Because he says that, we can have confidence.

But we are invited to be more than sheep.

As we follow Jesus, we are invited to live lives of faith like the exemplary shepherd. We're invited to follow where the good shepherd leads us and to lead and serve like he did. We can't get anything done in God's world by charging off, hoping God's people will follow our powerful vision or our ten-point plan. We have to hang around with other sheep. The place where we communicate the grace of God is right in the middle of other sheep, mixing in with the world we hope to make better.

We follow the God revealed as the good shepherd, the shepherd who cares for the sheep, and he invites us to love in the same way. As sheep, we *are* stupid. We miss the grace of God over and over, miss seeing signs of love and forgiveness every day, and miss chances to take care of each other. And yet there is the good shepherd, always calling us back to the good water and the abundant grass, giving all that we need, never letting us wander too far. No matter how far we think we've wandered away, the good shepherd is there, watching out, ready to bring us back to the pasture. No matter how stupid we think we've been, the good shepherd awaits, and we belong to the flock. The shepherd knows the sheep, and our God knows us.

We are sheep, but also followers of the great shepherd. He invites us to care for the flock alongside him. The strength for that comes from the shepherd himself, right in the midst of us, the flock.

We, the sheep, may be stupid — but we are smart enough to know our shepherd, and to know where we belong. Amen.

Soul Testing Kits

In this Easter season, we return to the scriptures where Jesus is saying goodbye to the people closest to him. They happen before his death, but they also have special meaning in the Easter season. Soon, the people who followed Jesus were going to have to live without him in their midst, in the same way that we do. We live with his resurrected presence. Here, he was giving them instructions about how to live in the world without him right there. Jesus was speaking, and he said:

John 15:1-8

'I am the true vine, and my Father is the vine-grower. He removes every branch in me that bears no fruit. Every branch that bears fruit he prunes to make it bear more fruit. You have already been cleansed by the word that I have spoken to you. Abide in me as I abide in you. Just as the branch cannot bear fruit by itself unless it abides in the vine, neither can you unless you abide in me. I am the vine, you are the branches. Those who abide in me and I in them bear much fruit, because apart from me you can do nothing. Whoever does not abide in me is thrown away like a branch and withers; such branches are gathered, thrown into the fire, and burned. If you abide in me, and my words abide in you, ask for whatever you wish, and it will be done for you. My Father is glorified by this, that you bear much fruit and become my disciples.

A friend of mine, happily married for 25 years or so, has moved a number of times for her husband's work. Every time they move, they look at houses together. He diligently checks for the right number of bedrooms and bathrooms and evaluates how long the drive to work is. She looks at how the light falls, how the rooms flow together, how the house "feels" to her.

She can't understand how he could possibly consider some places just fine, and he's baffled about why she's turning down perfectly good houses. Perhaps this happens in your family, too.

Each of them wants to be sure the house will be a happy home for their family, and each of them thinks something different will make that happen. And maybe each of them is right. For him, if there are enough bedrooms and bathrooms, then the love of the family will make it a happy place to be. For her, if the light falls right and the tree outside is welcoming, then everyone will feel good in the house, and it will become a home for them.

Who knows?

The process of becoming at home someplace is different for each of us. As I look back at the places I've lived over the years, the happiness I felt in each place didn't have much to do with bathrooms. An apartment in Washington, DC, after college, full of the energy and excitement of the city, where I lived with a dear friend, now gone on to heaven. The first house my husband and I lived in after we were married was a drafty rental house, with a basement so filled with spiders that we finally closed the door and left it to them …but we could hear the sound of the ocean waves at night, and smell the sea on the wind. Our next house was a tiny little bungalow, but our days were filled with the sweetest little baby ever.

Many of us will live in different apartments, houses, senior-residences, and even nursing homes over the years. Each place tells us something about our lives. The house where we raise the kids. The house we move out of, when it becomes too big. The house where we finally get the garden just the way we want it. The house where we remember the magic of childhood — or its terrors. The house of the unhappy marriage. The house where we face illness. The house we can't afford but buy to impress someone. The house where we never feel safe.

Jesus was talking about another kind of home in this passage, when he said, "abide in me." Live in me, he said, and he wants us to know that our true home is in him. This passage comes right after the familiar words we hear often at funerals, where Jesus comforts his friends by assuring them that in God's house, there are many dwelling places, or mansions, or a home for everyone. He continued that idea here, assuring us that we are rooted in God. Our deepest home is in the home of the divine, the heart of love, the place of infinite grace.

Jesus said an interesting thing about God here. He told us that this is not a God who demands, who is angry or vengeful, or who offers harsh judgment. This is a God who wants connection to humankind. This is a God who invites us to come home, and rest.

Jesus told us about the life of community here, too. We are all tangled up with each other, just like vines who twist around each other and can't be separated. As Gail O'Day wrote about this passage [in the *Interpretation* Commentary]: "To live as the branches of the vine is to belong to an organized unity shaped by the love of Jesus. The individual branch is subsumed into the communal work of bearing fruit..." In other words, if you won't want to bear fruit, that's not just about you — it matters to everyone because we're all connected as branches on the same vine. What each one of us does matters to everyone else here.

Just like "home" feels different for each one of us, the connection with God is different for each one of us. We have the same root, and we are different branches. Some of us find God in silence ...or in the beauty of hiking or camping ...or in the still, quiet moments of the morning. Others of us hear God clearly through other people or see God's energy when people work together on projects. Others of us see the tenderness of God as we teach Sunday school, serve meals, or sit next to a small person and read a book. Still others know that the voice of God sounds through music.

We change over time, too.

Our branches grow and we need different things. We have the same root in God, but we grow in different ways. For myself, the older I get, the more I long for times of silence to listen for God speaking and know that I have to build those into life. I'm sure you've seen changes in your own connection with God over time, too.

Recently, I was out driving around in the country, and I may have been driving a little too fast because I passed a store advertising — I swear — "Soul Testing Kits." What would be in a soul testing kit, I found myself wondering? Hardship, which tests the soul, for sure — or loss? Realizing we're not who we thought we were? There might be disappointing behavior from other people or being on the receiving end of lies and betrayal. It coul be discrimination or a time when God feels distant, and we struggle to get the connection back.

That's the pruning that Jesus is talking about — the life events and experiences that cut away our false selves, test our character and reveal our flaws. Life prunes us all, and we can become bitter and resentful, or we can use it for growth. The events that shape our spirits, rein us in or stretch us are the very things that make for growth. God comes along, too, to prune out the old habits that don't work anymore, or the character flaws that get in our way.

God who won't leave us like we are. Where we need it, God will come along to trim us and prune us, to make us grow better and more abundantly. You wise gardeners already know how that works. It's hard to believe that cutting off something perfectly good will make the plant healthier in the long run. You can't even tell right away, either. Between the pruning and the growth, there's a long time of trust ...or worry ...until something new begins to grow.

I suspect that's another part of abiding in Jesus. We come back there to rest after being pruned by life. We can stand the pruning process because we know where we belong, and know we have a home in God. We know that God is growing something in us, and so we can embrace the snipping and cutting and stripping away, knowing that we will bear more fruit afterward.

And so, following the resurrected Jesus, we make our home in God.

We are rooted here, welcomed here, and can rest here. In this home, we are fed for the work of serving the world. Of all the places we will live over the years, nothing can match this home. This connection with the Risen Christ is our truest, and most lasting home, the place where we always are at home.

In Jesus' name, Amen.

John 15:9-17

When It's Good, It's Really Good

We continue hearing Jesus speak about how we should live in the world and remain connected to him, even without his immediate presence. He was talking to his disciples here, and we listen in, for words that apply to us, too.

John 15:9-17

As the Father has loved me, so I have loved you; abide in my love. If you keep my commandments, you will abide in my love, just as I have kept my Father's commandments and abide in his love. I have said these things to you so that my joy may be in you, and that your joy may be complete.

'This is my commandment, that you love one another as I have loved you. No one has greater love than this, to lay down one's life for one's friends. You are my friends if you do what I command you. I do not call you servants any longer, because the servant does not know what the master is doing; but I have called you friends, because I have made known to you everything that I have heard from my Father. You did not choose me but I chose you. And I appointed you to go and bear fruit, fruit that will last, so that the Father will give you whatever you ask him in my name. I am giving you these commands so that you may love one another.

In her lovely book, *When the Heart Waits*, author Sue Monk Kidd told about a time when she was pregnant with her second child. Her son, Bob, was three at the time, and scared of the dark. He often called out to her in the middle of the night. "One night," she says, "as I held him to comfort him, he asked, 'Mama, is it dark in there where [the baby] is?'

'Yes,' she answered, 'it's dark in there.'

'He doesn't even have a nightlight does he?' [her little boy asked.] 'Do you think he's scared all by himself in there?'

'I don't think so,' she answered, 'because he's not really alone. He's inside of me. And it's the same way with you. When it's dark and you think you're all by yourself, you really aren't. I carry you inside of me, too. Right here in my heart.'"

She went on to say: "We need to remember that we're carried in God's divine heart, even when we don't know it, even when God seems far away."

Abide in me, Jesus invites us, and he tells us that when we do that, we are surrounded by love.

Mother's Day calls us to remember the places where we have been blessed by love, and it also reminds us that no human love is perfect. For some of you, Mother's Day and Father's Day are happy days. You have been blessed by a loving family, and this is a joyful day. For others of you, these are painful days. Perhaps you're waiting to become a parent, and the wait is long. Or, the perfect families of the commercials seem so distant from the parents you got. You feel the absence of the parent who died young, or who was never really able to be a parent. Everyone else seems to have the perfect family, and our lives look all the more flawed on days like these. Even in the most loving families, no mother or father can do everything. Even the most devoted parent has lapses and gaps in their love.

We need other connections to fill in the gaps, add to the foundation, make us whole. We need our chosen family, or church family, or mentors and wise guides, to fill the spaces.

My own thoughtful and conscientious parents never saw a need to tell me or my brothers when they thought we had done something well. It seemed to go without saying, for them. When I was in high school,

I had occasion to have lunch with my pastor, and he said to me, "Your mother is so proud of you."

"Really?" I asked him, genuinely shocked. "Are you sure? My mother?" It was complete news to me.

Now, I tell my daughter whenever I notice something that I'm proud of in her …but there are other things I miss, other gaps that will have to be filled in by other people. There are things she will have to receive or learn from other people — as we all do.

Love comes to us in many forms, all imperfect until we meet God face to face. What we don't find in one place, we gain from another. Our connections to each other are deep and lasting, but there are always things to be filled in by partners and friends, colleagues and teachers, friends from church. We find a home in many relationships, and each one makes us more than we would be otherwise.

In the deepest relationship of all, Jesus invites us to abide in him. God's love always fills in where we need it and holds us in God's heart.

The deepest home of all is wherever we are deeply loved.

Years ago when the space shuttle Columbia broke apart on its return journey, and the astronauts were lost, *The New York Times* reported that the family members of the crew had been waiting in Florida for the shuttle to land there. They waited as the time for the return came and went …with their anticipation changing to anxiety, and then to fear. When it became clear that something was very wrong, NASA officials rushed the family members away, and put them on a plane for Houston. At that point, the families knew that the astronauts must be gone, but nothing else.

Later, they learned that the shuttle had broken apart around the Texas-Louisiana border, but no one knew that then. Still, when the NASA plane carrying the families reached that place in its flight, Iain, the eight-year old son of astronaut Laurel Clark, started waving out the window.

What are you doing, his father asked him?

"Waving goodbye to Mommy," he answered, "I felt her [here]."

A year later, on the anniversary of the crash, his father took him on a vacation to the beach. Iain spent the afternoon stamping out, "I love you, Mommy," in huge letters in the sand. "Do you think Mommy can see that from space?" his father asked him.

"Of course not," he answered with all the wisdom of a now nine year old. "It's too far. But she can see it from heaven."

For better or worse, we leave our imprint on each other. Some imprints are joyful, and endure forever. Others leave behind a footprint of pain. Most are both. Our connections with each other are mysterious, and love comes in many forms.

Deeper still is our connection to the God who loves us always. We abide in God's embrace from the beginning of our days to the very end. Jesus invites us to make our home in him, and to grow from that root to love one another.

We are always in the heart of the God who loves us with the passion and wisdom and fire of a mother, as of a father. We are always and forever at home in the God who loves us. Amen.

Can I Get A Witness?

As you all know, one of the pleasures of being part of a group —
a family, a sorority or fraternity, or a church — is the ability to share
memories with each other. We get to live through our experiences again
through the memories, and other people fill in details we missed at the
time. You know this happens with friends, or civic groups, or church
friends. "Remember when…?" someone starts, and then everyone
chimes in with parts of the memory.

Each memory sparks another one, adding to the pile of stories.

But it also reveals that we never remember quite the same things.

Even siblings, in the same family, recall things in different ways.
Our memories merge and blend or fade away.

In this story, Jesus was counting on his disciples to remember. He
built it into their faith from the start. They had to remember so they
could keep telling the story. "You are my witnesses," he said.

That's frightening.

Eyewitness testimony used to be the gold standard in court, and now
we know how flawed it is. We know how imperfect, how faulty, how
full of holes our memories are. How can we possibly be witnesses for
Jesus when we can't remember what we wore yesterday, or who texted
us an hour ago?

Memory can be a soft welcome, or a sharp barrier.

It can either include or exclude.

When we assume everyone has the same memories, we leave people
out. When we say, "The church used to…" we leave out all the people
who've come since that time. When we say "We always…" we leave out
the people who are doing it for the first time. When we say "Everyone

knows me," the new person will slip away in shame that they don't.

Christian memory always includes people. "This is my body, given for you," Jesus said, and he meant not just the people around that first table — and not just the people around our table …but everyone who came along. When we hear "you are a chosen people," it means claimed, not the kind of chosen that leaves everyone else out.

"You are my witnesses," Jesus said, and he counts on us to tell his story.

This is not because we have perfect memories - not because we have perfect lives, even, but our lives serve as our witness.

Our evangelical friends have an idea of witnessing to people, which means actively telling about our faith. Some people have a gift for that, and some people don't. Some people want to hear and some people don't.

Our truest witness is how we live. It's not what we say …people forget that. It's how we spend our money, supporting the things we believe in. The tone of voice we use with strangers, or people who have fewer resources or lower status than we do, in the way we seek honesty and fairness at work, in the way we spend our time, in the way we speak up to call out a demeaning joke or an act of aggression, in the way we tell the truth, even when it's inconvenient.

When I think about the people who have witnessed to me, it's not the talkers I remember. Occasionally, it's something someone said. Most often it's the example they gave me, not for my benefit, but for their own.

When I was a hospice chaplain, in my early years of ministry, one of my patients was a man named Mr. Low. He was an exceptionally quiet man, near the end of his life when I met him. His wife, Mrs. Low, was a small, round woman who talked enough for both of them. She had gaps in her teeth, and holes in her stretched out shirts, but the brightness of her smile made you forget all of that.

They lived in a battered house on a quiet street in a town that had seen much better days. I would climb up the front porch steps, which were slowly rotting away, and go into the living room, which was stacked high with things Mrs. Low thought she might need some day ... or things someone had given her, that she planned to give to someone else. Each month it was a struggle to pay the rent. Mr. Low was too sick to work, and Mrs. Low stopped working at the deli when her feet hurt too much.

Some days there was enough, and other days, she wondered how they would have enough to eat. Somehow, in spite of that, or because of it, she had the most vibrant faith of anyone I've ever known. If someone brought them dinner, or a bag of bread, she saw it as a direct gift from God. If the day was hard, she knew God would make it better. If she had more than enough of something, she would give the extra away, trusting that God would bring more when she needed it.

Mrs. Low never asked for anything for herself, but she was never shy about asking for something for her church. If the True Vine Baptist Church needed chairs, or a new bus, or flowers for a Mother's Day program, she would call me up, fully trusting that I would give her whatever I could.

I think now about how little I really understood her struggles, but she took me and all my naiveté under her wing anyway. When her husband died, she sent a note to my boss saying that we were going to be friends for life ...and we were, until the time of her death. Of all the hundreds of hospice families I've known, maybe thousands, I've stayed in touch with only a handful ...and she chose me, for some reason.

Mrs. Low, with the gaps in her teeth and in her education, taught me something about faith, and trust, that I couldn't have learned from someone with more resources. Her life, and her prayers, were a witness to the power of God through all kinds of adversity. Her complete trust in God stays with me, still.

Our lives are our witness. Someone is always watching. A student in our class, wondering what they want to be like when they're an adult ...a neighbor, who's in a hard place ...a grandchild, who doesn't go to church because church doesn't mean anything ...someone in our community group, who quit church years ago.

Someone needs our example, just as we need theirs. We do this together, as a community, filling in the gaps in each other's faith.

"You are my witnesses," Jesus says. He could find someone more perfect, someone more educated, someone more successful, someone with better words to say, but he chooses us.

So then, may our lives reveal his story.

In Jesus' name, Amen.

Seventh Sunday of Easter

John 17:6-19

Gifts You Can't Return

As we near the end of the Easter season, we hear Jesus speaking as part of his farewell message to his disciples. He originally spoke these words just before his death, to prepare his friends. These same words have the same special resonance for us now. The disciples have to learn to live in the world without Jesus' physical presence, just as we do.

We listen in, as Jesus spoke to God about his followers.

John 17:6-19

'I have made your name known to those whom you gave me from the world. They were yours, and you gave them to me, and they have kept your word. Now they know that everything you have given me is from you; for the words that you gave to me I have given to them, and they have received them and know in truth that I came from you; and they have believed that you sent me. I am asking on their behalf; I am not asking on behalf of the world, but on behalf of those whom you gave me, because they are yours. All mine are yours, and yours are mine; and I have been glorified in them. And now I am no longer in the world, but they are in the world, and I am coming to you. Holy Father, protect them in your name that you have given me, so that they may be one, as we are one. While I was with them, I protected them in your name that you have given me. I guarded them, and not one of them was lost except the one destined to be lost, so that the scripture might be fulfilled. But now I am coming to you, and I speak these things in the world so that they may have my joy made complete in themselves. I have given them your word, and the world has hated them because they do not belong to the world, just

74

as I do not belong to the world. I am not asking you to take them out of the world, but I ask you to protect them from the evil one. They do not belong to the world, just as I do not belong to the world. Sanctify them in the truth; your word is truth. As you have sent me into the world, so I have sent them into the world. And for their sakes I sanctify myself, so that they also may be sanctified in truth.

When my daughter was a tiny baby, premature and reluctant to join the world, my parents came to visit. The baby came home from the hospital, and our world exploded with activity, uncertainty, and a distinct lack of sleep. Like many people, I found it all overwhelming. Somehow, they had let me bring this tiny baby home from the hospital …it seemed impossible to believe. I was pretty sure there was some huge mistake. I was trying to take care of the baby and the house, and I somehow felt a need to prove to my parents that I knew how to be a good parent.

I would spin through the house, full of anxiety, and from time to time my dad would disappear. I always found him sitting by the baby's crib as she slept. In that cloud of uncertainty, he would take a few moments, just to sit, and I always knew that he was praying for the baby. Maybe even for me, too, his own sleepless, overwhelmed baby.

He got what I was missing in my sleepless, anxious haze. This time was a gift. This tiny human being was a gift …as we all are.

Those prayers — along with many others — have continued to cast a net of care around that baby, who is now in college. Her early years were cushioned by the prayers of her grandparents, along with those of parents and friends.

In a similar way, Jesus was building a wall of care around his disciples as he prepared to leave their presence. They would have to live in the world in a different way, without his daily guidance, without his wise and fiery presence, without the compassion of his touch.

As Jesus talked to God about his disciples, he conveyed that he found them to be a gift from God. "You gave them to me," Jesus said. When we read the gospels, we know that the disciples are, at different times, clueless, vengeful, self-serving, and silly, all mixed in with their love for

Jesus. They were not so different from us. After traveling around with them, seeing their mistakes, seeing how slow they were to understand, he could have been saying to God, "Here they are. I've suffered these fools long enough." But no, Jesus still saw them as a gift.

If Jesus saw these first disciples as a gift, it gives me hope that he sees us a gift. Even though we, too, are at times, clueless, vengeful, self-serving, and silly, mixed in with our love for Jesus.

And, if he sees us as a gift, we can see each other that way.

Author and professor David Fitch wrote about finding God's presence, and God's people at his local McDonald's. He started out by drinking coffee, and concentrating on grading papers, doing research and having meetings. The McDonald's was an extension of his office, and he set the agenda. Then a friend of his issued a challenge. The friend suggested that he see the local McDonald's as a place where God was already at work, apart from anything he was doing. He said, "I was challenged to see this place as a vibrant arena where God was truly present. I was exhorted to enter this place peacefully and be present with every person who came my way, pay attention to all that was going around me, and tend to God's presence here."

He changed his routine, and began to see the McDonald's differently. He looked up from his computer and his paperwork to see what was going on around him. He said, "As time went on I started to meet an array of people in surprising conversations. I got to know people struggling to hold onto a job, abused by a spouse, or mistreated by police. I got to know some police themselves. I shared tables regularly with people who lived in cars and vans. I became enmeshed in a network where God was working in people's lives, and I was swept up into it. I had never been invited into the lives of so many people as I was at this McDonald's (not even in a church)... I found myself joined with people in prayer, reconciliation, healing, and proclaiming the hope of the gospel. I became a participant in God's work. I was learning how to be faithfully present to his presence. I was catching a glimpse of what faithful presence might look like in the world... I now believe every neighborhood, coffee shop, community center, Black Lives

Matter protest march, YMCA, workplace, racial reconciliation village hall meeting, prison, city hall, homeless shelter, MOPS group, labor union hall, and hospital is a potential arena of God's presence similar to McDonald's."[1]

Jesus invites us to get out in the world and find him there, too. His living presence is in the classroom and the office presentation, at the bus stop and on the subway. He's waiting at the library and the bowling alley and the VFW hall.

This is the last Sunday in the Easter season, this is the time of year when we spend all these weeks thinking about the resurrection. This is the season of God's triumph over the powers of indifference and apathy, over death and destruction, over loneliness and isolation. God's power lives in the connections between people. God is present in the people we love, and in the people we find annoying, in the people we fail to notice at all.

And all of it is a gift, as Jesus reminds us.

Through the power of the resurrection, Amen.

---

1   David Fitch, *Faithful Presence: Seven Disciplines That Shape the Church for Mission* (Illinois: InterVarsity Press, 2016), 11-12.

www.ingramcontent.com/pod-product-compliance
Lightning Source LLC
LaVergne TN
LVHW091208080426
835509LV00006B/892